The Wing

Written and illustrated by
Ray Buckley

Abingdon Press

Nashville

The Wing

Book design: R. E. Osborne

ISBN 0-687-09704-5

02 03 04 05 06 07 08 09 10 11 – 10 9 8 7 6 5 4 3 2 1
Printed in Hong Kong

For Judy Weidman, Alma Snell, and Della Waghiyi

In many Native cultures, one's name reflects a spiritual identity. It can be a name shared by an ancestor of good character, or derived from a spiritual dream or vision. It may be a name reflecting a sacred vow or goal. In many traditional cultures, an individual's name could be changed by the community as a way to recognize a significant life-changing event. Spiritual change was marked by a change in identity.

When the circumstances of our lives are not changed, it does not mean that healing is not occurring. Often the healing is one of the spirit, changing the heart when the circumstances are not changed. Often the Creator, in an ongoing act of creation, changes our name. We are not always repaired. We are sometimes re-created.

The butterfly is a symbol of new life in both Native and Christian traditions. It is reflected in the Fancy Shawl Dance of Native women. In this story the butterfly is used to illustrate the quiet, unseen work of the Creator, always present, always active. Nothing touched by the Creator is left unchanged.

There was a wood, vast and wide, with tall trees that remembered when the Creator walked among them. In the wood lived the People whom the Creator had fashioned from the Earth. There were the Two-Leggeds, and the Four-Leggeds. There were those that flew with wings and those that crawled with many legs. In the whole of the wood, all creation lived as the Creator intended.

There was a small bird in the wood. She would dart among the trees, her feathers catching the light and sending it back again to amuse Grandfather Sun. Often, when the dew hung on the tips of the spruce needles, she would brush them with her wing, sending them twirling and sparkling in the light.

Turning low, she would fly beneath them, catching them on the tip of her beautiful beak. So great was her speed that the People named her She Who Flies Swiftly.

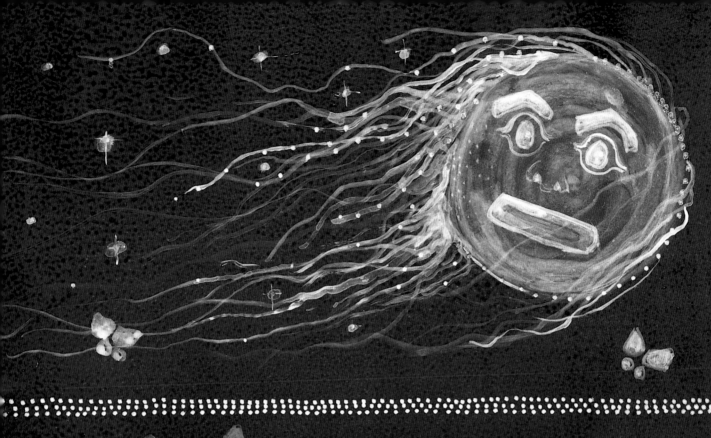
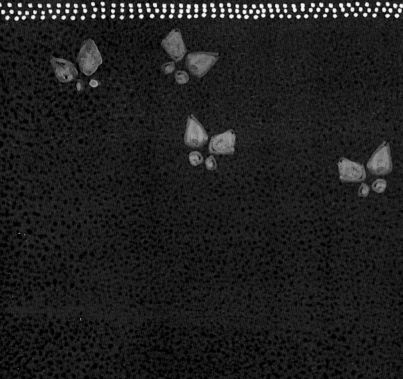

When Grandmother Moon had gone to her rest, and Grandfather Sun had begun his walk, She Who Flies Swiftly was not to be seen. The dewdrops watered the Earth without interruption, and the leaves rested undisturbed.

And when the Creator walked through
the wood, on the Earth was the form of She
Who Flies Swiftly.

Carefully the Creator lifted the little bird.
The hands which had formed the world
touched the small body until they found
in one small wing, a broken bone.

Gently the Creator touched the wing, and
laid She Who Flies Swiftly under the Great Tree.

The Two-Leggeds and the Four-Leggeds said, "How wonderfully she will fly. She has been touched by the Creator!"

And the People of the wood came to see her beneath the Great Tree, and She Who Flies Swiftly sparkled, even in the shade of the tree.

Days passed and the People of the wood gathered to see the bird fly again. Preening her feathers, she stood in the middle of the gathering and with her head high, leaped into the air. The Wind caught her body and one wing, but the broken wing did not open, and She Who Flies Swiftly fell to the Earth.

Why can't she fly?" the People murmured, "She's been touched by the Creator!"

"Perhaps she has offended the Creator!" one of the gathering cried.

"Perhaps she was never touched by the Creator!" another said.

And She Who Flies Swiftly was left alone, under the branches of the Great Tree.

More days passed. Grandmother Moon looked down upon the little bird. Grandfather Sun shone light into the wood, which only made the shadow of the Great Tree deeper.

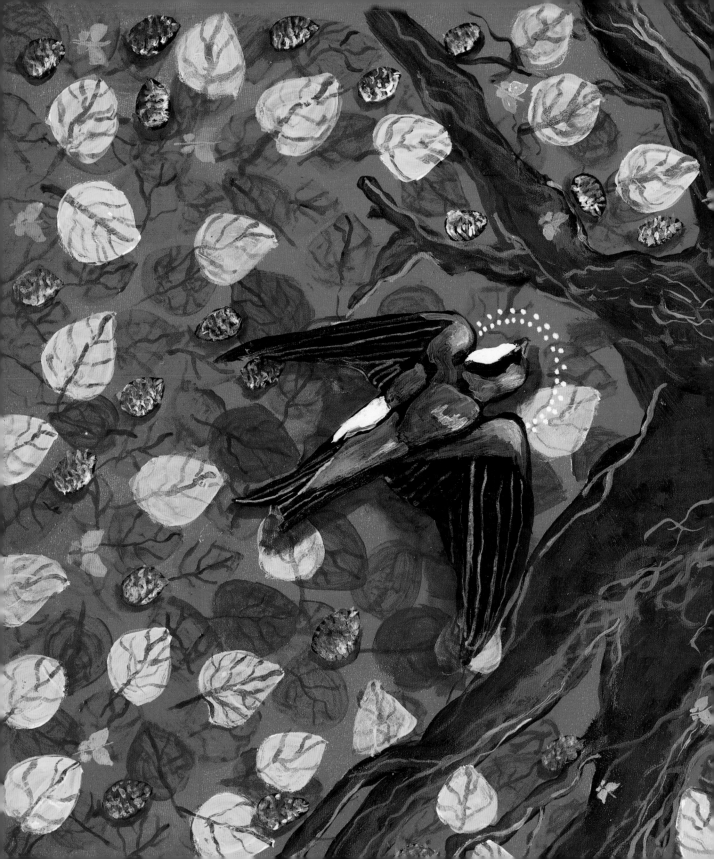

She Who Flies Swiftly walked around the tree, unable to fly. The People of the wood came to stare. And then they didn't come at all.

She Who Flies Swiftly sank into herself. The dewdrops sparkled to get her attention, but she could only see the shadows.

"Why couldn't the Creator fix me?"

"Help me!" she cried. There was no answer.

"Why can't you fix me?" she wept. Only the leaves of the trees answered.

Day after day, night after night, She Who Flies Swiftly shouted at the Creator. But the Creator was silent and did not walk in the wood.

"Perhaps I should ask more quietly," she thought, and low sounds came from her throat. Day after day, night after night, She Who Flies Swiftly sang. And from her broken wing and broken heart came notes of pleading. Notes of sadness. Notes of incredible beauty.

The People of the wood, the Two-Leggeds and the Four-Leggeds, came to hear the music. Those That Fly rested in the trees.

She Who Flies Swiftly sang. Still more People came. Lost in her song to the Creator, the bird did not see them.

But something had changed. The music was not always sad. At times it was nearly joyous, lifting and arching in the air. At times low and gentle, resting on the rocks and the moss.

And when it seemed that the music could not be more lovely, a sound like none had ever heard was added to the music of the bird. Quietly at first. Then strong and assured, and above all, loving, came the voice of the Creator.

In the evening, with the People gathered around, the Creator and She Who Flies Swiftly sang a duet. For an instant the People bore witness to the meeting of two hearts; one mighty and one small.

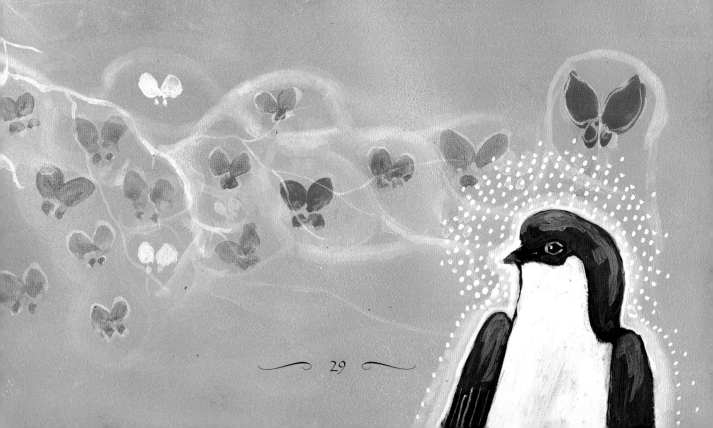

But She Who Flies Swiftly did not notice. She was singing. And the voice which the Creator had developed in her lifted above the wood.

When Grandmother Moon has put Grandfather Sun in his lodge and the wood is still, a song can be heard. It comes from beneath the Great Tree. It is a voice which came from a broken wing, sung by She Who Has Been Healed.

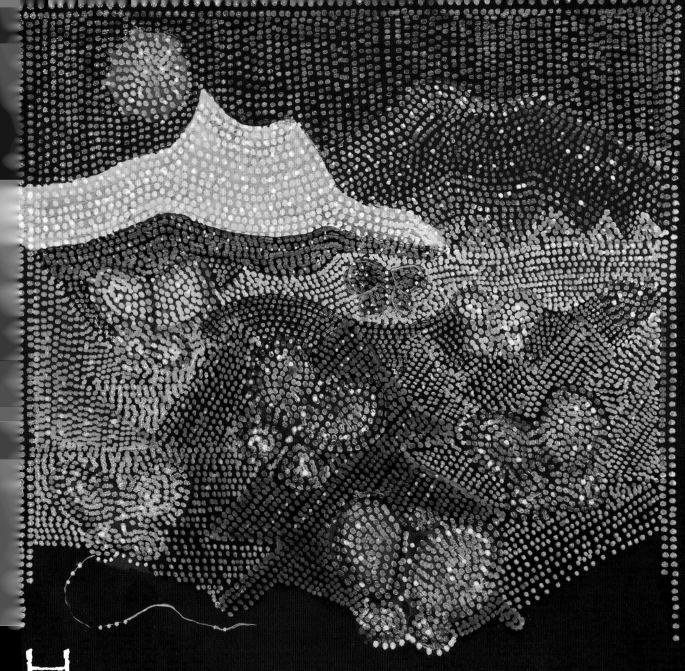

He heals the brokenhearted, and binds up their wounds.